The babysitter

Story by Beverley Randell

Illustrated by Ernest Papps

One day Mom had to take Baby Emma to the doctor. Nana went too.

Poppa was the babysitter
and he stayed with Tom.
They had fun playing with a ball.

Then the ball went up
on the roof.
"I can get it down," said Poppa.
"Get me a stick, Tom."

Tom went to find a stick,
and Poppa climbed up the ladder.

The ladder slipped, and Poppa fell. *Crash!* He hit his head.

"Poppa!" called Tom. "Wake up!"
But Poppa stayed very still.

Tom ran inside.

He ran to the phone.

He called **911**.

In an Emergency

Dial 911

Fire
Ambulance
Police

Do you want Fire, Ambulance, or Police?

Ambulance.

Ambulance here.
Do you want help?

My Poppa
fell off a ladder.
He won't wake up.
His head is bleeding.
I'm all by myself.

Where do you live?

6 River Road,
Homewood.

Tell me your phone number.

It's 555-0123.

Tell me your name.

I'm Tom Cook.

The ambulance is on its way.
Good boy, Tom.
You stay there.

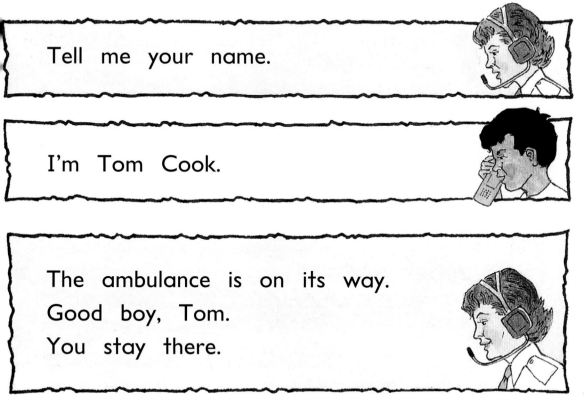

The ambulance came.

Poppa woke up slowly.
"Where am I?" he said.
"Did I fall off the ladder?"

"Yes," said the ambulance driver.
"Now you are going to the hospital.

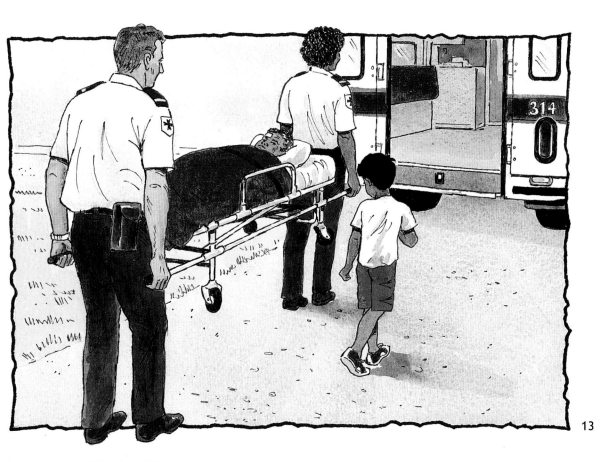

Mom and Nana
came home with Emma.
Mom saw the ambulance.
"**Tom**," called Mom. "**Tom**!"

"I'm all right, Mom," said Tom,
"but Poppa fell off the ladder.
I had to call the ambulance!"

"Tom had to look after **me**," said Poppa.

"Tom is a very good babysitter."

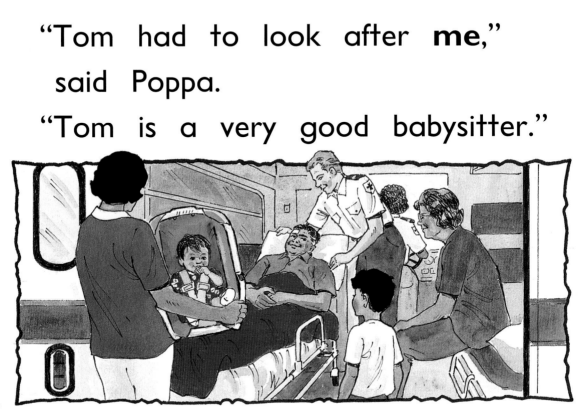